Household Hacks

150+ Do It Yourself Home Improvement & DIY Household Tips That Save Time & Money

By Ace McCloud

Disclaimer

The information provided in this book is designed to provide helpful information on the subjects discussed. This book is not meant to be used, nor should it be used, to diagnose or treat any medical condition. For diagnosis or treatment of any medical problem, consult your own physician. The publisher and author are not responsible for any specific health or allergy needs that may require medical supervision and are not liable for any damages or negative consequences from any treatment, action, application, or preparation, to any person reading or following the information in this book. Any references included are provided for informational purposes only. Readers should be aware that any websites or links listed in this book may change.

Table of Contents

DEDICATED TO THOSE WHO ARE PLAYING THE GAME OF LIFE TO

WIN

KEEP ON PUSHING AND NEVER GIVE UP!

Ace McCloud

Be sure to check out my website for all my Books and Audio books.

Introduction

I want to thank you and congratulate you for buying the book, "Household Hacks: 150+ Best Do-It-Yourself Household Tips and Hacks; DIY Home Improvement Hacks That Save Time and Money." This book contains proven steps and strategies to help you make your home a pleasant, safe place to live and entertain guests, all while minimizing your costs.

Take a look under your kitchen sink and notice how many commercial cleaners you have down there. I'm guessing you'll find dish soap or dishwasher detergent, along with an array of window cleaners, counter cleaners, drain cleaners, furniture polishes, carpet fresheners, carpet cleaners, and floor waxes. Stroll over to the laundry room and you'll find even more commercial products. Why do you think we lock these products away from our children and put Mr. Yuk stickers on them? Yes, because they are toxic. My question to you is: why do we keep toxic chemicals around our house?

If you think these chemicals are the only way to have a truly clean house, think again. I know, some of the commercially released "organic" and "environmentally friendly" cleaners just don't cut the mustard (or the grease), but you don't have to resign yourself to living in either a toxic environment or a clean one. There is another way.

It is possible to maintain your home without using toxic chemicals. It'll save you money, too. You don't need an array of poisonous chemicals to keep your house brand-spanking clean. What you do need is a few simple items. Vinegar, baking soda, salt, lemon juice, some hydrogen peroxide, borax and a few other much less lethal items than you're used to can work every bit as effectively as their toxic counterparts. Making your own cleaning solutions and finding simple ways of keeping your house orderly will offer a safe environment to anyone who visits your house.

I have a friend whose daughter could not even enter a place where certain chemicals – found in antibacterial cleaning sprays, no less – were used. She was highly allergic. If her skin touched a surface that had been wiped down with it, she would break out in hives. If she breathed the chemicals in, her throat would start to close up. She was pretty much limited to staying in her own environmentally safe home.

Most kids do not have allergies this severe, but her example should tell you something, namely, that many commonly used products are not safe for any child or adult. Unfortunately, we live in an age where you pretty much have to make your own cleaners if you want to know exactly what you're using. Nonetheless, that can be a good thing.

The process of making your own products will take a little of your time, but the payoff is significant. In addition to minimizing your family's exposure to dangerous toxins, you help save the health of the environment, you minimize the amount of waste that goes into our landfills, and you save money, to boot.

Several of these tips and tricks have been around for a long time, long before our ancestors could buy them pre-packaged in a store. Sometimes convenience isn't the best thing for us. Taking the time to make cleaners may take a little extra effort, but it is worth it in the long run. You can rest assured that you are exposing your family to only the best and healthiest products.

This book is not just about making safe cleaning solutions. I've also included suggestions for keeping your house orderly. You will find tips on storage strategies, organizing closets and pantries, keeping your environment smelling nice, and saving money on some of those little things you use for the upkeep of your home.

Once you try some of these tricks and tips you won't want to buy commercial cleaning items again, nor should you have to. You should be able to easily get the most out of fewer trips to the store, reduce your lifestyle expenses, and maintain a safe and clean home for your family and friends to enjoy.

Chapter 1: Make Your Own Cleaning Solutions – It's Easy

This chapter details some homemade cleaning solutions you can use every day. They are assembled easily in your own kitchen using common ingredients. You will find additional recipes throughout this book, but we'll start with the basics essential to every household.

Ingredients

Most of the ingredients I will mention can be readily obtained from a grocery store or a local pharmacy.

Here are the basic items you will need. With few exceptions, you can make everything you need out of one or more of the following:

- Vinegar

- Baking soda

- Salt

- Lemon juice

- Cheap vodka (the cheaper the better)

- Hydrogen peroxide

- Borax

- Rubbing Alcohol

- Dawn dish detergent

- Castile soap

- Washing soda

The only ingredients you are likely to be unfamiliar with are Castile soap and washing soda. Both of these items are usually located in the laundry detergent section of a grocery store. Washing soda can also be found occasionally in a hardware store.

Castile soap originally had an olive oil base. It was first made and sold in the olive-rich Castile area of Spain, hence the name. Today, Castile soap is made using any vegetable-based oil. The solid form – which I recommend using – is semi-hard and white in color. It grates easily and is useful in the making of cleaning solutions. Dr. Bronner's and Kirk's are the major manufacturers of Castile soap, which is readily available in most grocery stores.

Washing soda is similar to baking soda, with only a slight difference in its chemical makeup. It is an alkaline substance that removes stains from fabric and permeable surfaces. It is not a soap. It can remove scale from coffee machines; it can strip floors and remove stains from clothing. It is a skin irritant, so care must be taken when handling this substance.

Washing soda can be hard to scare up sometimes, but you can make your own with minimal effort. If you can't find the stuff anywhere, you can easily convert baking soda into washing soda, just by baking it.

Hack #1 – To make washing soda, preheat your oven to 400 degrees Fahrenheit and sprinkle **baking powder** over a shallow baking pan with edges; a jelly roll pan or cookie sheet will work fine. Bake the stuff for half an hour, stirring every 10 minutes or so to ensure that it cooks evenly. When it looks less fluffy and more like salt, you will have achieved the transformation. The resulting substance should appear fine-grained, dull, and opaque. You don't want it to turn brown; it should remain white in color.

Dedicated Equipment

It is always best to reserve specific bowls and utensils for making household cleaners. Never use them for preparing food. The processing will leave some residue and your brownies won't taste very good with soapy overtones, will they? When it comes to grating Castile soap, use a grater dedicated to that purpose alone; otherwise you can only imagine how your cheese will taste!

It is best to use glass bowls and metal spoons instead of plastic or wood. These will last indefinitely, as long as you don't break the glass. No need to buy anything super-expensive; run-of-the-mill equipment will work just fine for our purposes. After all, cost savings is part of the advantage of making your own cleaners.

Hack #2 – All-Purpose Cleaner

Ingredients:

- Baking soda

- White vinegar

- Water

Equipment:

- Glass bowl

- Measuring cups

- Stirring spoon

- Funnel

- Spray bottle

- Glass jar (optional, for storage of excess)

Every kitchen needs an all-purpose cleaner; this one is made with baking soda, vinegar, and water. Never buy a small box of baking soda; always opt for the big boxes because you will use them up quickly. The best thing about baking soda: it is quite inexpensive, so don't hesitate to buy plenty.

To make a general cleaner, put 1/2 cup of **vinegar** in a bowl and add 1/4 cup of **baking soda**. Keep your face out of the bowl, because this will foam up a bit. Mix it well, then add 1/2 gallon of **water**. Pour this into a spray bottle. You can store the excess in a glass jar if you have extra.

Before you use it each time, give the spray bottle a shake. You can use this to clean counter tops, stove tops, faucets, tables, chairs and anything else you would spray with a general all-purpose cleaner.

Hack #3 – Antibacterial Cleaner

Ingredients:

- Water

- Borax

- White vinegar

- Tea tree oil

Let's say you want a cleaner with more antibacterial power. Place 3 cups of hot **water** in a large spray bottle and add 2 teaspoons of **borax** and 4 tablespoons of **white vinegar**. Vinegar by itself will kill most germs, but to make the antibacterial solution longer lasting, add 3 drops of **tea tree oil**.

This can be sprayed on counter tops, toilets, sinks, door knobs or wherever germ-laden hands will touch.

Hack #4 – Disinfectant Spray

Ingredients:

- Vodka

- Distilled water

- Essential oils (rosemary, eucalyptus, wild orange, or tea tree)

You can make a great disinfecting spray using vodka. I get the cheapest vodka I can find. It isn't the best-tasting stuff, but it does make a great disinfectant.

You can add essential oils to unleash more cleaning power. Rosemary is an antimicrobial. Eucalyptus, is a germicide. Wild orange discourages the growth of bacteria, as does tea tree oil.

To make this spray, mix 1/2 cup **vodka**, 1/2 cup **distilled water**, and the following amounts of one of the following essential oils:

- 15 drops of rosemary

- 20 drops of wild orange (or tea tree)

- 10 drops eucalyptus.

Essential oils can be found in grocery stores, some pharmacies and most health food stores and vitamin shops. They make things smell good while they kill germs.

Put the resulting solution in a spray bottle and shake before each use.

Hack #5 – Glass Cleaner

Ingredients:
- 70% Isopropyl (rubbing) Alcohol

- White vinegar

- Water

Glass cleaner doesn't just clean windows. It also makes microwaves, glass stovetops, and glass tables sparkle.

Mix 1/4 cup of **alcohol** in a spray bottle with 1/2 cup of **white vinegar** and 2 cups of tap **water**.

The vinegar cleans windows and mirrors of dust, oils, and other grime while the alcohol causes the solution to dry quickly so it won't leave streaks. Place the mixture in a spray bottle and spritz it on your windows. Do not use paper towels to wipe this off as it will leave little bits of towel and streaks behind. Instead use black and white newspaper or coffee filters for a clean, smudge-free shine.

Hack #6 – Wall And Baseboard Cleaner

Ingredients:

- Hot tap water

- Borax

Equipment:

- Gallon milk jug

- Funnel

- Spray bottle(s)

Feel like getting into the nitty gritty of cleaning house? Here is a wonderful cleaner that will make your wallpaper or paint look like new again. It is easy to make and works like a charm.

You will need a spray bottle and a couple white cloths to do this job. Cloth diapers or old white T-shirts work the best. Once you are done, just throw the cloths in the laundry so you can use it over again. This will save money you would spend on paper towels, which you shouldn't be using for this anyhow. Paper towels will leave a gritty residue on your walls.

Clean out an empty gallon milk jug and fill it almost to the top with hot **water** from the tap. Pour in 1/2 cup of **borax**.

Borax is usually found under the name "20 Mule Team Borax." It can be found with other laundry items in the grocery store. I have occasionally found in a hardware shop, as well.

Borax is a powder, so you will need a funnel to get it into the opening of the jug. Once well dissolved, pour the mixture from the jug into a spray bottle. The substance is most effective when warm, but it'll clean pretty well when cold, too.

Simply spritz the mixture on the wall and wipe it off. You'll want to start at the top and work your way down toward the baseboard. Spritz and wipe. Borax has a nice clean smell and it will make the house feel much cleaner.

Hack #7 – Floor Wash

Warning: Do **not** use on wood or marble flooring.

Ingredients:

- Warm water

- White vinegar

Make floor wash by filling a bucket almost full with warm **water** and mixing in 1/4 cup of **white vinegar**. Mop the floor with this combination. For really messy stains, like spilled jam or dried-on food, bring along a scrub brush to lift them off. Spills should come off easily after wetting them down.

Never use this floor wash on wood because it will strip the finish right off. Also avoid using it on marble flooring because it will make the marble look dull and lifeless.

Hack #8 – Vinyl And Linoleum Cleaner

Ingredients:

- Warm water

- Vinegar

- Borax

- Baby oil

Put 1 gallon of warm **water** (minus about 2 cups) in a jug or bowl or and add 1 cup of **vinegar**, 1/4 cup of **borax** and 2 drops of clear **baby oil**. Don't slop this on the floor with your mop because it can be dangerously slippery. Instead, pour the solution into a spray bottle, then spritz and mop a section at a time. If the floor feels a little slippery after it dries, just mop it again with a little warm water in a fairly dry mop.

Hack #9 – Wood Floor Cleaner

Ingredients:

- White vinegar

- Vegetable oil (NOT olive oil)

- Water

I did not forget about your wood floors. Wooden floors call for special care. Too much moisture can warp a wood floor and cause real problems.

For this reason, you will want to put the cleaning solution in a spray bottle and work your way from one corner of the floor to the next, spraying and mopping a section at a time, instead of slopping liquid all over the floor. Only spray enough to moisten the floor and get the dirt up. Rinse your mop periodically in hot water, but wring it as dry as possible.

To create an excellent wood floor cleaner, combine 1/2 cup **white vinegar** with 1 teaspoon **vegetable oil**. Don't use olive oil, because it will make the floor even more slippery than the vegetable oil, and yes, it will be slippery while it is wet. As it dries, the vegetable oil will soak into the wood and moisten it, making it glisten. Mix the vinegar and vegetable oil with 1 cup **water** and if desired, add 5 drops of a preferred **essential oil**. I like citrus, eucalyptus, or lavender for a clean, fresh scent.

Hack #10 – Abrasive Scouring Powder

Ingredients:

- Washing soda

- Salt (non-iodized)

- Essential oil (optional)

- White vinegar

If you use an abrasive cleanser on your sinks, make your own and save tons of money. Mix 1/2 cup of **washing soda** in a large bowl with 1/2 cup **salt** and 1 cup **baking soda**. Do not used iodized salt; the iodine just doesn't work well. In fact, I prefer sea salt or kosher salt because the granules are a little coarser than with regular salt. You can also add 5 drops of a favorite **essential oil** for fragrance. Mix it all together and pour into a lidded glass jar or a glass cheese shaker. If you use a mason jar, take the lid and make holes by pounding a nail repeatedly through it so the powder can come out when shaken.

To use, first wipe the surface you are cleaning with some **white vinegar**. While it is still wet, sprinkle on the powder. Wait 5 minutes, then scrub with a brush and rinse. You will be surprised at how well this works.

Hack #11 – Soft Scouring Paste

For a softer touch that won't scratch, grate 1/4 cup of **Castile soap** into a bowl. Add 3/4 cup of **baking soda** and 1 tablespoon of tap **water**. When you pour in 1 tablespoon of **white vinegar** it will foam up a bit. You can add a few drops of **essential oil** to make it smell better, if you wish. Store any excess paste in a jar with a tight fitting lid. Whenever you need a non-scratching abrasive cleaner, just scoop out a little onto a wet surface and scrub away. If you don't use it quickly enough, the paste will mold, in which case you can just throw it out. I never let it go that long, however, because I use it all the time; it's my standard cleaner for a fiberglass shower surround and the accompanying metal sink.

Chapter 2: Kitchen Hacks That Work

Your kitchen needs to be one of the cleanest areas in your house. The food you prepare here will pick up any contaminating substances and can easily cause harm to both family and guests. A clean kitchen is important to the safety of your whole house.

Most of the solutions already described can be used in the kitchen. The cleaning hacks in this chapter will concentrate on some of your kitchen appliances, as well as on pots, pans and other items used in the line of cooking. I have included some food management tips to help keep your family safe from food poisoning and to simplify kitchen cleanup.

First we will cover some kitchen cleaning hacks.

Hack #12 – Dishwasher Detergent

Ingredients:

- Borax

- Washing soda

- Kosher salt

- Citric acid

You do not need fancy dishwasher powder, liquid, or gel to get your dishes clean as a whistle. Take a large wide-mouthed glass jar and pour in 1 cup of **borax**, 1 cup of **washing soda**, 1/2 cup of **kosher salt** and 1/2 cup of **citric acid**. (Citric acid can be found in your local pharmacy and in stores that sell canning supplies.) Cover the jar and shake it well to mix everything up.

When you're ready to wash your dishes, scoop out 1/4 cup of the mixture and put it in the detergent compartment. Wash your dishes as you normally would.

Hack #13 – Dishwasher Cleaner #1
Ingredients:

- Borax

- Water

A dishwasher does tend to get a little dirty after a while. It might even look a little moldy around the seal. To stop this, sprinkle 1/2 cup of **borax** in the bottom of the dishwasher after doing a load so that the compartment is still a little wet. Leave it overnight. After about eight hours, go back and wipe everything down with a damp rag, especially around the seal.

Hack #14 – Dishwasher Cleaner #2

Ingredients:

- White vinegar

- water

You can also run a cycle with 1/2 cup **vinegar** in the reservoir and no dishes in the dishwasher. This will clean the washer and leave it smelling fresh.

Hack #15 – Dish soap

Ingredients:

- Boiling hot water

- Borax

- Castile soap

- Essential oil

Let's say you have no dishwasher. No problem! You can make a dish soap that powers through grime and grease and leaves your dishes squeaky clean. In a glass or ceramic bowl, pour 1-3/4 cup **boiled water** and add 1 tablespoon **borax** and stir it until it dissolves. Mix in 1 tablespoon grated **Castile soap** and include a few drops of a favorite **essential oil**, just for the clean smell. I like citrus scents in my kitchen.

Stir this potion until the soap melts. Store it in an empty plastic or glass bottle and give it a shake before pouring into your sink to do the dishes.

Hack #16 – Sparkling Glass Rinse

Ingredients:

- Vinegar

- Water

Sometimes you may notice that your drinking glasses have become a little cloudy and dull. They no longer sparkle and shine. This can happen whether you are washing them in a dishwasher or by hand.

There is an easy remedy to this problem; it is called vinegar. Measure 1/4 cup of **white vinegar** and pour it on the bottom of the dishwasher. Proceed to wash the dishes. Another method is to put the vinegar in a sinkful of water and wash and rinse the glasses by hand. Let them air dry and your glasses will shine.

Hack #17 – Cleaning The Microwave

Ingredients:

- Vinegar

- Water

I don't know about you, but my microwave gets really cruddy over time. Things spill and spit; the appliance is used so frequently that we seldom take the time to wipe it out.

One solution is to put a mugful of **water** with a tablespoon of **vinegar** added and microwave on high until it boils. Let it boil until it really steams up the cooking compartment. Press "Stop" and let things cool down a bit, then wipe out the microwave with a soft, moist rag. The steam will loosen all that crud so that it comes out pretty easily.

Another solution is to dampen a cellulose sponge with **water** and place it in the microwave. Spray the inner chamber all over with a mixture of equal parts **vinegar** and **water**. Run the microwave on high for 2 minutes, then let it cool. Before anything can dry by itself, take the sponge and wipe out any debris for a clean-as-a-whistle microwave.

Hack #18 – Grease Remover

Kitchens tend to be a bit on the greasy side. Grease piles up on the stove, on the wall behind it, and travels farther than you would imagine. My collection of beautiful glass jars sets about eight feet from my stove. I have to take those jars down at least two times a year and wash the grease off. You could be the cleanest person in the world and still have a grease problem in your kitchen. If you think grease is easy to remove, think again, but there is a solution.

To adequately cut through grease you need a substance called sudsing ammonia. This product is simply regular ammonia that has a detergent added. Fill a gallon container, or your kitchen sink, with warm water and add 1/2 cup of **sudsing ammonia** To protect your skin from ammonia's irritants, wear rubber gloves when washing off the grease Avoid inhaling the fumes, too. Ammonia can burn your lungs if you aren't careful. However there is nothing better than this to get rid of grease. You can immerse a sponge in the solution and wash off your stove and the wall behind it or you can wash glassware and dishes in it. Rinse everything well.

Non-toxic Grease Remover

If you're looking for a non-toxic way to remove grease, the following solutions can work as effectively as the more toxic ammonia:

- **Hack #19** – Boiling water is often all you need to lift off grease. A soft rag or scrubbing sponge dipped in **boiling water**, combined with a little elbow grease, will take off most light greasy coatings.

- **Hack #20 – Vinegar** will also break down grease so you can wipe it off more easily. The most effective application is via a spray bottle. For stubborn grease, spray on full-strength vinegar; for lighter layers, dilute the vinegar in half with water. Spray it on, let it set for a few minutes, and then wipe it off. The vinegar smell will dissipate in about thirty minutes.

- **Hack #21 – Baking soda**, when mixed with **vinegar**, creates a chemical reaction that can help remove more stubborn grease. First spray vinegar on the greasy surface, then sprinkle on it the baking soda. Keep your nose away from the resulting bubbly mess. Once the reaction has simmered down, get in there with a scrubbing sponge. The baking soda has a slightly abrasive quality that you can use to scrub away baked-on grease.

Hack #22 – Cleaning Greasy Pots And Pans

Grease on pots and pans makes a real mess. Not only does it not come off easily, preferring to leave a nasty residue, but you have the chance of dropping your pans because the grease can make them slippery.

This remedy works well on metal and glass pans and casserole dishes. Note: DO NOT USE THIS METHOD ON NON-STICK POTS AND PANS; it will scratch off the finish. Sprinkle the offending surface liberally with table **salt** while the pan or dish is still hot to warm. Let it sit for 1 hour then dump any loose salt into the garbage and clean the pot. This method is good for aluminum, stainless steel, glass, and cast iron.

Remove Burned-on Food

Food that has been burned into the bottom of a pot, pan or casserole dish is usually very difficult to remove. Many people just give up and throw away the blackened pot. However, I've discovered two methods that actually work! These can be used to restore your favorite pots and pans to normal condition.

- **Hack #23** – Cover the blackened bottom of the cookware with warm water and add 1 cup of **white vinegar**. Put it on the stove and bring it to a boil. Remove this from the heat and add 2 tablespoons of **baking soda**. Let it sit and do its thing for 5 to 10 minutes, then pour out the liquid and scour clean, rinsing with warm water. The burned food should release easily from the surface of your pan.

- **Hack #24** – It sounds odd, but this second method involves the use of a dryer sheet (you know, the anti-static-cling sheets you toss in when you dry your clothes). Pour in a cup of **vinegar** and cover the offending substance with water, then lay a **dryer sheet** on top of it all. Let this set overnight. The next day, discard the dryer sheet, pour out the liquid and any black stuff that remains should wipe out easily. Note: Some cases will need longer than a one-night-stand.

Hack #25 – Oven Spills

Nothing is worse than food spilling over in the oven and creating enough smoke to set off your fire alarm every time you turn on the oven. Should something spill while you are baking, immediately throw some table **salt** over the spill on the oven bottom. This will stop the smoking and will let you keep on cooking. Later, after the oven has cooled, wipe the salt out with a damp sponge. The spill should clean up easily.

Hack #26 – Rust Spots On Stainless Steel

I tend to get rust spots on my stainless steel silverware. I hate those little brown marks that show up on my knives and spoons, going do so far as to throw them out because I just don't want to put them in my mouth. However, I finally got tired of throwing away my utensils and learned how to remove those ugly spots.

What I discovered works on anything stainless. I don't usually buy bottled **lemon juice**, because I prefer the flavor of fresh lemons, but in this case I buy a large bottle of the stuff. For utensils, I lay them flat in a shallow pan and cover them with lemon juice. With a pan, I just prop it so that lemon juice can cover the rust spot. Let the stainless sit for 10 minutes, then scrub and rinse. The rust will be no more.

Hack #27 – Cleaning Your Sponges And Scrubbies

I dislike sponges in the kitchen because I tend to see them as nasty germ collectors. However, I also hate to fill up landfills with paper towels. The solution? I found a way to keep my sponges and non-metal scrubbies clean and germ-free (at least until I dirty them again).

Every night, before I run the dishwasher, I put my sponges and scrubbies in the top rack along with the dishes. They come out clean and fresh ready for another day.

Hack #28 – If you're not into running your dishwasher that frequently, I've also moistened my sponges with **vinegar**, put them on a plate and heated them for a minute in the microwave. The vinegar kills germs, as does the heat. As a bonus, the steam created in the process will make it easier to clean your microwave, if you're so inclined.

Hack #29 – Marble And Granite Cleaner

Marble and granite counter tops require special care and cleaning. I've already warned you against using several homemade solutions on them. Marble and granite can scratch and easily become dull or discolored. Because the stone is not cheap to replace, you need to use special care when cleaning it.

Here's what I recommend for your stone countertops. Take a clean, empty spray bottle and pour in 1/4 cup of cheap **vodka**. Add three to 4 drops of a non-citrus-scented, clear **dishwashing liquid**, along with 5 to 10 drops of a non-citrusy **essential oil**, such as lavender or rosemary. Fill the rest of the spray bottle with water. Shake the bottle first, then spray and wipe down your countertops for a shiny finish.

Hack #30 – Stainless Steel Appliance Shine

Stainless steel appliances can also lose their shine fairly easily. A good way to restore the sheen is to pour a few drops of olive oil on a soft white cloth and use it to wipe them down.

Hack #31 – Cutting Board Cleaners

You would not believe how much bacteria can collect on a cutting board. I love wooden cutting boards, but I never use them for meat. Instead, I get thin plastic sheets designed for cutting. They are easy to store but ensure that there is no chance I can hurt my countertops. I use a green sheet for beef, blue for fish, a clear sheet for chicken and a pink one for pork. You can clean these cutting sheets in your dishwasher or immerse them in water with a little **vinegar** added.

Hack #32 – I still use the wood board for cutting vegetables and fruits. After use I wipe it down with equal parts **vinegar** and water and let it air dry. This effectively kills any bacteria lurking in the pores of the wood.

Hack #33 – Prevention – Slick Down Your Measuring Cups

I often cook with honey and molasses and these things can stick and make a mess in your measuring cups. One surefire way to cause sticky ingredients to slip right out of measuring cups is to first coat them with nonstick **oil** spray. I've also learned to measure my oil in the cup before measuring sticky liquids; the stuff then slides right out.

Hack #34 – It's Too Salty

Have you ever gotten carried away and dumped too much the salt in your soup? Here's a tried and true remedy to reduce the saltiness. Simply peel a **potato** and toss the whole thing in while your soup cooks. The potato will absorb the extra salt and you just throw it away before serving. Your soup or stew will taste delicious. Of course, if you *really* overdid it...maybe two potatoes are in order.

Hack #35 – Boiling Over

I have a frequent problem with pots of pasta, soup, beans, etc. boiling over and spilling their contents all over the stove. It makes for a messy cleanup and wasted food. However, I have that problem no more, thanks to an old remedy from pioneer days.

The pioneer women prevented massive boil-overs by laying a **wooden spoon** crosswise atop the rim of their soup pot. Of course, you want to ensure your spoon is not too close to an open flame; we don't want to serve up spoon flambé.

If you do it right, the wooden spoon will break the bubbles as they rise, releasing steam into the air instead of carrying liquid over the side of the pot. Thanks to the physics of bubble-bursting evaporation, your pot will not boil over.

Hack #36 – No More Stinky Onion Hands

If you visit my kitchen you will find an oversized **stainless steel spoon** setting on my countertop. This was one of my grandmother's serving spoons, but I don't use it to serve food.

When you cut onions, the smell permeates your hands and even though you try to wash them, you can still smell like an onion for hours. When I finish cutting onions, I now wash my hands and while they are wet I grab that old spoon and rub it all over my hands, including between my fingers. The result: no more onion smell. I can't explain it; I just know it works. After using it, the spoon doesn't smell like onions either.

I recommend watching a humorous YouTube video called "10 Brilliant Kitchen Hacks" by Quest Nutrition. In addition to making you chuckle, you'll discover even more tips for cooking and kitchen cleaning .

Chapter 3: Inexpensive Family Room Hacks

Outside of the kitchen, which is where my family hangs out most of the time, the living room – or family room – is usually the heart of the home. This room may contain carpet, tile, upholstery, wood, vinyl, plastic, metal, glass and other substances, all of which need to be cleaned and maintained regularly. In addition to adults, this can be a high-traffic area for kids, so you want the area to be not only clean but nontoxic. The following tips and hacks address these needs and can help make the family room a safe place for even crawling infants.

Hack #37 – Carpet Freshener

No one likes a stinky carpet. If you have kids and pets, you know that carpets can harbor distasteful smells for a long time. **Baking soda** is known for soaking up smells in your refrigerator, but you can also use it safely on your rugs. Just sprinkle some on the carpet and let it set for 5 to 10 minutes before you vacuum it up. The results: a fresher-smelling room. Don't go too wild with your sprinkling or you'll have a real mess on your hands. Just sprinkle enough that you know it is there.

Hack #38 – Carpet Stain Remover

Never install light to medium colored carpet if you have kids and pets. I have learned my lesson; let's leave it at that. Even dark carpet shows up some dirt and stains. At any rate, you'll need these hacks if you have any carpet in your home.

As with any stain remover, you'll want to test these solutions before using them on a stain. Find an area that won't be easily seen. Because some types of carpet – especially wool – may not respond well, or a solution may fade the carpet fibers, you want to try it out before using a solution in a conspicuous area.

I am an expert at getting stains out of carpet – after all, I have the carpet I warned you about – so this is how I do it. Combine **white vinegar** and **distilled water** in equal parts in a spray bottle. Every time you get a stain on your carpet, first blot off what you can with a paper towel and then spray it. Let this solution rest on the carpet for 10 minutes or so, then take a scrub brush dipped in tap water and scrub the spot. Blot the spot again and the stain should come out, unless it is one of those stubborn stains you encounter occasionally. But I have a solution – or two – for even those recalcitrant stains.

Hack #39 – Stubborn Stain Remover#1

I would still test this first, applying it in an unobtrusive corner, and leaving it on for 10 minutes to see if any fading occurs. If all is well, put 1 cup of lukewarm **water** into a bowl and add 1 teaspoon of a **clear dishwashing liquid** (the kind without lotion).

Scrub this into the stain. It will foam up but just keep scrubbing and blotting, each time using a fresh section of a light-colored cloth towel. I keep several white hand towels handy just for cleaning my carpet. Once I've used them, I toss them in the wash so they'll be ready the next time I need them. With my gold carpet, I need them a lot.

Hack #40 – Stubborn Stain Remover #2

This stain remover involves applying a tablespoon of **regular ammonia** mixed into 1/2 cup of warm **water**. This may make your eyes water if you get too close, but dab it on the carpet with one of your towels and it should take the stain right out.

Hack #41 – Upholstery Cleaner

The fabric that covers your chairs and sofa is different from both carpet and your drapery. Chairs and sofas are some of the most frequently used furniture in your house, so you can count on needing to clean and de-stain them periodically.

I know this sounds repetitive, but it is important to test any of these fabrics before you use them on a broad scale. A test on an unseen corner will assure you that the solution will not fade, disintegrate your upholstery, or make the colors run.

You will want to minimize how wet you get your upholstery. Underneath that fabric is soft stuff that can take forever to dry; it can also be dissolved by some cleaners. Instead of dousing and blotting, as with carpet cleaning, you want to keep wetness to a minimum when working with upholstery.

To make a general upholstery cleaner that brightens and brings newness back to your upholstered furniture, mix 1/4 cup of clear, non-lotioned **dishwashing liquid** with 1 cup of warm **water**. Put this in a glass or metal mixing bowl and turn on the electric mixer to make it very frothy.

Before applying, vacuum your furniture well to get rid of any loose debris, including pet hair. Apply the froth with a soft scrub brush or a white cloth and blot immediately with another white cloth. The dirt you have extracted should show up on your blotting towel. Work methodically, spraying then blotting one small section at a time.

Hack #42 – Upholstery Stain Cleaner

When your upholstery is stained, first blot the stain with a soft cloth. Anything that soaks into the chair or sofa will call for a little extra work.

To make an upholstery stain cleaner, mix 1/2 cup of **cornstarch** with 1/2 cup of **baking soda** in a bowl. Make a paste by adding a little water. Apply the paste to the stain and leave it alone until it dries. It is important to cover the stain with the paste, but don't pile it on several inches high, because you want it to dry in thirty minutes to an hour. Carefully scrape off the paste after it is dry. The stain should come with it. Vacuum up any remaining debris.

Hack #43 – Furniture Polish

I like to make my own furniture polish because it does not cake up as thickly as the commercial brands and I can choose any scent I want. This solution makes my furniture glisten. First, remove any dust with a microfiber cloth. Microfiber traps dirt, dust, and debris; it will make the wood ready to receive the polish. You don't want to polish in any of the unwanted crud, so remove it before you proceed.

You probably won't use all the polish up at once, but it will keep for several months. Mix 2 drops of **lemon oil** with 1/2 cup of warm **water** in a spray bottle. The trick is to spray the mixture directly onto a soft cloth and rub it into your furniture. Never spray it directly onto the wood. The process of rubbing it in will leave the wood shiny.

Hack #44 – Water Ring Remover

It doesn't seem to matter how many times I ask people to use the coasters prominently placed around the house; I'll walk into the family room and see three sweating glasses sitting on antique wood tables, with lovely white rings developing beneath them. Fortunately, water rings are easy to remove.

Take some **mayonnaise** and gently work it into the ring on the wood. Don't rub too hard, but make sure it saturates the area where the ring lies. Use a white cloth to rub the area and you will see the ring disappear before your very eyes. You can also use **toothpaste** for this task but avoid whitening toothpastes. Some types of toothpaste tend to take the shine off the wood, so be careful.

Hack #45 – Wood Restorer

Sometimes your wooden furniture gets a little dull and lifeless. When this happens, I turn to tea bags to bring back its life. Steep 4 **black tea bags** in 1 cup of boiled water and let them set there until cooled. I wouldn't drink this as it will definitely put hair on your chest.

Remove the tea bags and put the liquid in a spray bottle dedicated solely for this purpose. The tea will cling to the bottle, staining it, but that is okay. Spray the liquid on a cloth rag, which will also be stained forever. Never spray this right on the wood. Wipe down the wood furniture with the cloth and let it air dry. The tannins in the tea will remove any old polish that is dulling the wood and you will be left with a brilliant shine. Be careful about using this on very light woods and never use it on unfinished wood.

Hack #46 – Keep Track Of Remotes

Remote controls seem to delight in getting lost. It is very easy to knock one off the coffee table or forget you left it in a chair. I have cats that play at night and are constantly knocking items off or pushing them under furniture.

The solution to this problem is to attach **Velcro** strips near where you watch television. Stick the other side of the strip on the back side of your remote. When not in use, anchor the remote to its designated spot using the Velcro. The next time someone wants to watch TV, they just unstick it.

Hack #47 – Designate A Play Area

Many times a children's play area will be located in the same place as the television, so that playing tends to encroach upon a person's television watching. I suggest you designate an entirely separate play area, marking it off with colorful **carpet squares** or by using flooring made of interlocking foam puzzle pieces. Another option is to put down a colorful **area rug**. Whatever you use, make this area the special place for the kids to use when playing with their toys. When they are finished, the toys are left only in the carpeted space. This will minimize the chance of trips and falls over toys in a more high-traffic area of the house.

Hack #48 – Make A See-Through Walled Play Area

You can easily mark off a play area using **bookshelves**. Just ensure that the shelves are anchored to a wall or to the ceiling; you don't want children in their climbing stage to be able to pull the shelves down on themselves. If you have no wall handy against which to anchor your bookshelves, you can always drop a wire down from the ceiling joists and suspend them that way.

I recommend using shelves that have no backing. This way, you can easily see around the shelves to monitor your children at play.

Hack #49 – Unconventional Coffee Table

Extra storage is always useful in the family room. You might have video games, magazines, newspapers, blankets, or craft projects that need a place to be stashed when not in use. I use a **steamer trunk** as a coffee table; the lid serves as the top of the table. I keep my knickknacks on a tray atop the trunk, cum table, making it a simple matter to lift off the tray for easy access to everything inside.

Hack #50 – Storage Tub Tables

When I was in college my roommate and I needed extra tables to put lamps on. With little money to go around, we bought some **storage tubs.** We used one on each end of the sofa and stacked two together to serve as a lamp stand. We covered the tubs with thrift store tablecloths and no one was ever the wiser. The best thing about these makeshift tables is that you can store stuff inside. You not only get nice end tables, you also add to your storage capacity.

Hack #51 – Suitcase Storage

Vintage suitcases are all the rage right now. You can store DVDs and video games in them and stack three or four in a corner.

Hack #52 – Basket Storage

Baskets can be a decorator's friend. They make stylish and artistic storage for blankets, toys, newspaper, magazines, etc. Baskets can often be slid under tables and chairs or behind sofas to add valuable storage space to a room.

Hack #53 – Speed Cleaning

You don't have to spend forever cleaning your house. The experts have all sorts of tricks. I recommend watching the YouTube video, "Clean Your Home In

Half the Time With These Hacks" from Money Talks News.

Chapter 4: Tips to Make Your Bathroom Sparkle

Who doesn't want a squeaky-clean bathroom? It needs to be clean for your health, as well as for the comfort of your guests. A dirty toilet is not just a health hazard; it also sends a strong negative message (read: "Yech!") to anyone who sees it.

Bathrooms offer some unique cleaning challenges. Humidity from the shower can foster the growth of mold and mildew throughout the room. The tub can hold its own convention of griminess. The toilet can become particularly nasty, chrome faucets can grow unsightly mineral deposits, sinks can harbor messy toothpaste droppings, and the mirror can collect spatters from all sorts of anonymous sources. The following are some tips on how to keep your bathroom sparkling without devoting your whole life to the project.

Hack #54 – Toilet Bowl Cleaner

I do not like the gel type toilet bowl cleaners. Sure, they stick to the sides of the bowl and run down them, but it takes elbow grease to get that slimy blue or green stuff to come off. Fortunately, there is a much better way.

First, flush the toilet. Then, sprinkle a quarter cup of **baking soda** around the sides of the bowl, above the water line. Follow that with a quarter cup of **vinegar**. Close the lid and let the mixture stew for about 15 minutes. The chemical reaction between the soda and the vinegar will create a foam, but this is normal.

After 15 minutes, use your toilet brush to clean above the water line and under the edges of the bowl. Then flush and you will have a sparkling clean – and sanitized – toilet bowl.

Surprising Toilet Cleaners

Believe it or not, these two products can clean a toilet better than any gel toilet solution ever could and you can often find them in dollar stores for half price. **Hack #55** – Drop in a couple **Alka Seltzer tablets**, the plop, plop, fizz, fizz stuff, and watch them go to town.

Hack #55 – The same thing happens with **denture cleaning tablets** that fizz in water; they can clean a toilet until it sparkles. Just drop two tablets in and let them fizz away. After a few minutes, scrub and flush.

Hack #57 – Toilet Freshener

This toilet freshener spray can be used every other day or so, just to keep germs from taking over your toilet. The main active ingredient, **tea tree oil**, is a powerful disinfectant. Put 2 teaspoons of tea tree oil in a spray bottle, along with 2 cups of water. Shake, then spritz the toilet seat, under the seat and inside the toilet near the rim.

Let this sit for 15 minutes, then wipe with a damp cloth outside the toilet and with the toilet brush inside. In addition to killing germs, this will keep the toilet smelling fresh and looking good.

Hack #58 – Soap Scum Scrub down

Soap scum has a tendency to collect on glass shower doors. The best way to get rid of it is to take a dryer sheet (the kind you put in with clothes to keep static clean away), scrunch it up and rub the glass doors with it. Do not wet anything; just rub it while dry and it will take the soap scum right off.

Remove Rust Stains

Hack #59 – You can use the **abrasive scrub** or the **soft scrub** (Hacks 10 and 11) from the kitchen section of this book to clean bathroom sinks and tubs. Some water types will leave rust stains in your sinks and tubs. To remove rust stains, put some scrubbing solution on the stain, let it set for a minute, then scrub it off with an abrasive pad.

Hack #60 – For stubborn rust stains, make a paste from **baking soda** and water. Apply this to the stain, let it set for 15 minutes, then scrub it off.

Hack #61 – If this doesn't do the trick, go to a hardware store and buy a **pumice stone**. Wet it and rub the stone directly on the rust stain. Small pieces of pumice will come off and form a paste-like substance. Let this set for 10 minutes or so and then scrub it off.

Hack #62 – Sparkling Chrome

Chrome faucets can become cloudy and scaly in a bathroom. To restore their luster, take a bit of toothpaste (about the size of a dime) and rub it on the chrome. Buff this off with a soft cloth. Now you should be able to see your face in the chrome!

Hack #63 – De-clog Your Showerhead

Over time, your showerhead can become clogged; some of the little holes either don't work anymore or they spray water at crazy sideways angles. Too keep your showerheads flowing freely, I recommend treating them at least 4 times a year, as follows:

- Put about a cup of **apple cider vinegar** into a small zip lock bag. (Note: white vinegar can be used as well. Both vinegars will lose their smell after about thirty minutes of exposure to the air.)

- Place the bag over the showerhead, submerging the head completely.

- Zip the bag closed and secure it with rubber bands.

- Let the showerhead stew in the bag from an hour to overnight, if it's in really bad shape.

- Remove the bag and wipe off the outside of the showerhead.

- Turn on the hot water and let it run for a minute. Your showerhead should no longer be clogged.

Hack #64 – Tile Cleaner

Bathroom tiles tend to become dull over time, so this should brighten them up. Wipe – or spray – the tile surface with some **white vinegar** and while it is still damp, pour a little **baking soda** on a damp rag and wipe those same tiles again. To remove the soda residue, wipe down or spray the tiles with water. You should be able to see yourself in the clean tiles.

Hack #65 – Fiberglass Cleaner

Make your own version of bubbles that scrub away grime. You can use this to clean fiberglass and any other surface. This solution is safe to use anywhere in your bathroom.

Mix 1 cup of **baking soda** with 1 teaspoon of regular blue **Dawn dish detergent.** This will make a bubbly paste. Use a cellulose sponge to work the paste into the fiberglass. You don't have to work in sections, just keep working it in to the entire area.

Half fill a bucket with warm water and add 1 cup of white or cider **vinegar.** Use your sponge, dipped in this liquid, to wipe down the paste. Little dirt-fighting bubbles will quickly form. Once you are finished with the vinegar solution, turn on the shower and rinse everything down the drain.

Hack #66 – Grout Cleaner

Grout in the bathroom – and to a lesser extent the kitchen – can become discolored over time; it can also collect mold and mildew. To clean your grout, put 2 teaspoons of **cream of tartar**, found in the spice section of a grocery store, in a bowl and add enough fresh or bottled **lemon juice** to make a paste.

Take an old toothbrush and apply this paste to the grout, scrubbing vigorously. After a good scrubbing, wipe down the paste with a sponge dipped in clear **water**.

Hack #67 – Mildew Fighter

Mildew can gather in showers, especially in basements and non-vented rooms where the shower never really dries out. To prevent mildew from growing, fill a spray bottle with **water** and add 10 drops of **thyme essential oil**. Alternatively, you can boil a couple sprigs fresh thyme in 3 cups of boiling water for about 5 minutes before cooling and bottling it. After you shower, spray this solution all over the shower and just let it air dry. The thyme oil will prevent mildew from forming.

Hack #68 – Drain Cleaner

Drains in the bathroom are a tricky thing. Hair and soap tend to congregate in the drain and clog things up real good. This drain cleaner is designed to break up those clogs and clean out your bathroom drains. Practice preventative maintenance by performing this drain clean at least four times a year:

- Pour 1/2 cup of **baking soda** down the drain.

- Follow this immediately with 1/2 cup of **vinegar**. This will cause a lovely little chemical reaction that will dissolve hair and break up clumps of other stuff in the drain.

- Leave this for 15 minutes while you go boil a teakettle full of water.

- Pour the **boiling water** down the drain. .

Hack #69 – Mirror, Mirror On The Wall

You can clean your bathroom mirrors with the glass cleaner in the solutions section of this book, but if you want to prevent fogging when steam is released from the shower, rub non-lotion **shaving cream** on the mirror. Then wet a soft rag and wipe everything off. Your mirror should be fog-free for a week or so.

Towel Issues

Most bathrooms have just one or two towel racks. If you have a large family or frequent guests, that is nowhere near enough. Here are a few possible solutions you may find helpful.

- **Hack #70** – Get an old-fashioned wooden ladder and prop it against the wall at an angle. Voila! You now have a multiple-level towel rack.

- **Hack #72** – Affix multiple towel bars to the back of the bathroom door about 1 foot away from another. You should be able to get three towel racks on the back of a door.
- **Hack #73** – Hang coat-hooks across the bathroom door or along a wall space. Towels dry almost as quickly when hung on hooks as on a regular bar.

Hack #74 – Toiletry Storage

Place lidded glass apothecary jars on the vanity to hold cotton balls, makeup remover squares, and cotton swabs. Put a silverware utensil tray in a drawer to hold brushes, combs, nail clippers, tweezers, and other small toiletries. You might even be able to fit some makeup in there.

Hack #75 – Rust Rings On Countertops

Hair products and shave gel are often presented in metal spray cans. Because of the high humidity level in your bathroom, these cans may leave unsightly rust marks on your countertops. To prevent this from happening, take nail polish and paint it around the bottom edge of metal cans. Once this dries you can set the can on the countertop without any danger of creating a rust ring.

Chapter 5: Boost Your Bedroom's Ambience

Your bedroom should be your haven; it should be a place you can relax and unwind. Of all the rooms in your house, this one should be designed as an oasis of calm, restful, and restorative energy. Your bed should be comfortable, the air clean, and it should only contain refreshing sounds. Everything should be designed to give you a good night of sleep so you can go out there and conquer the world the next day.

The following tips will help you improve the environment in your bedroom. The organizational tips can make it easy to find what you need with minimal effort and time.

Hack #76 – The Headboard

Most beds have a headboard and some may even have a footboard. A headboard is useful to keep your pillows from sliding down onto the floor. Even if your bed frame is up against a wall, without a headboard your pillows can still slip down and end up under or beside the bed. A headboard also serves to keep the mattress and box springs aligned so the bed feels steady.

A headboard gives your bed a finished look and – on a practical note – it stops you from bumping your head against the wall (although it only softens the blow if your headboard is padded).

If you don't have a headboard, there are several easy ways to create one. You can recycle old doors, attaching one to the frame at the head of your bed. You can also take **plywood** in the shape of a headboard, cover it with **foam**, then staple **fabric** on top. Your bed will be much more comfortable and beautiful with a headboard

Pillow Talk

Hack #77 – Pillows get dirty quickly because we drool on them at night and they collect dust like a magnet attracts metal. For this reason it's important to cover your pillow with a washable pillowcase and replace it frequently. If you're sick, change out your pillowcases frequently to minimize the amount of germs you breathe in at night.

Hack #78 – Many people don't know that you can wash pillows. **Foam pillows** can be washed in the bathtub by hand. These pillows must be air dried, however, to slow the aging of the foam.

Hack #79 – **Polyester pillows** can be washed in the gentle cycle of your washing machine. Always wash two pillows at a time to keep the washer balanced. Let the washer's agitator cycle run for just two to three minutes, then rinse and spin the water out. Put the pillows in the dryer along with three tennis balls. This will help the pillows plump up as they dry.

Hack #80 – Down pillows can be washed, but they require special handling:

- Remove the pillowslip and pillow protector, if present.

- Examine the pillow closely for rips and tears. Any holes, tiny or otherwise, must be sewn closed before washing, to avoid a washer-full of feathers.

- Use a front-loading machine to avoid any damage to the feathers from a top-loader's agitator.

- Put the pillow in the washer with the long dimension facing the door. Always wash with either a second pillow or a couple of towels, to prevent excessive movement.

- Use **liquid detergent** and less of it than usual, because the stuff is harder to rinse out from a pillow. While you're at it, wash the pillow in cold water on the gentle cycle and rinse it twice, just to ensure you get all the soap out.

- If you're concerned about yellowing or stains, you can add 1 cup of **white vinegar** and 1/2 cup of **hydrogen peroxide** to the wash cycle.

- Run the spin cycle two times, to remove excess water and to extract any lingering soap residue.

- After washing is complete, extract the pillow, wrap it in a thick, dry towel, and press out what water you can. Warning: do NOT twist or wring the pillow.

- Place the pillow in the dryer with a couple of dry towels; they will absorb some of the pillow's moisture and even out the drying process.

- Add in a couple tennis balls to help fluff the pillow and break up clumps of feathers to facilitate drying.

- Dry on air only. Even low heat can be damaging to the feathers. This will take time, meaning several hours.

- Every forty minutes or so, take the pillow out and fluff it to break apart dense clumps of wet feathers and ensure even drying.

- Do not use the pillow until it is completely dry. If you want, you can hang the pillow outside on a line to finish drying and absorb some fresh air.

Hack #81 – Sleep-Enhancing Mini-Pillows

Make a sleep pillow by mixing some dried **lavender flowers** with a little **orris root**, a scent fixative you can find in many herbal or health food stores. Mix in 3 to 4 drops of **lavender essential oil**. Take a square of loosely woven fabric and sew around 3 sides to make a small pillowcase. Put your lavender potpourri in it and sew it shut. Slip this little pillow under the pillowcase near where your head will rest on the pillow. It will bring sleep quickly and can give you pleasant dreams.

Hack #82 – Bedding Storage

Keep extra sheets, pillowcases and blankets in plastic storage tubs. Throw in a scented dryer sheet – or a fragrant sachet – before sealing the lid and your bedding will smell fresh when you go to use it.

Hack #83 – As The Mattress Turns

Turn your mattress at least 4 times a year to maintain its shape and to prevent uneven wear. Mattresses are expensive, so you want yours to last as long as possible. I turn mine the first week of every quarter. I flip it from side to side and turn it from top to toe. Use this opportunity to vacuum under and around your mattress to get rid of any accumulated dust and dirt.

Hack #84 – A Safe Bed For Toddlers And Babies

What can you do for a bed when a baby or toddler spends the night and you don't have a crib? There is a solution. Insert a **pool noodle** under the fitted sheet on each side of the bed and at the head and foot. A toddler can probably crawl out, but will have to think about it first and a baby will not be in danger of falling off the edge of the bed.

Hack #85 – All The Pretty Closet Clothes

Most of us have outfits in our closet that we haven't worn in years. Here is a way to decide what to keep and what to get rid of. With the start of the year take out all your clothing and replace each item in the closet with the **hanger facing backwards**. After you wear something, hang it back up with the hook facing the normal direction.

In three months take a look at everything that's still on a backward hanger. If these clothes are seasonal, keep the hooks backward a little longer. Use this opportunity to note things you haven't worn in a while and get rid of them if you can. Gift them to a friend (somebody who'll appreciate the present) or donate them to a nonprofit thrift store.

Non-Slip Hangers

Hack #86 – Not too many people I know can afford those expensive hangers that keep your clothes from slipping off them. My simple solution is to coil a **pipe cleaner** around the slanted part of the hanger, covering the area where your clothes normally touch. The pipe cleaners help to grip the garment and keep it from falling off.

Hack #87 – If you don't have pipe cleaners handy, what about **rubber cement**? Brush a light coat on the top surface of the hanger, where your clothes will touch, and let it dry for 24 hours before using.

Hack #88 – Okay, so you don't have rubber cement, either. Surely you have **rubber bands** lying about. The fat ones work best. Just attach one to each "shoulder" of a clothes hanger to prevent your clothes from slipping off.

Hack #89 – Storing Scarves And Ties

Scarves and ties can be a tricky thing to store in a closet. One solution is to hang plastic **shower curtain rings** from the bottom rung of a plastic hanger. Ties can be hung through a curtain ring. Tie scarves loosely around a curtain ring so they will stay put. (Avoid knotting the ties on or they will wrinkle.)

Shoe Storage

Hack #90 – Ladies' shoes are easily stored by hanging two **tension rods** across the bottom of a closet. One will hook the heel at the back and the other will support the toe by placing the rod a little forward.

Hack #91 – Another way to store shoes with even a low heel, including men's shoes, is to nail some **crown molding** across the back of the closet and hang shoes from it by their heels.

Extra Storage

Hack #92 – You always need extra storage in a bedroom. You can get this by using **foot lockers, trunks, chests, and baskets** to store bedding, clothing and other necessities.

Hack #93 – You can also put your bed on **risers** to add enough height to store shallow plastic storage bins underneath. Slide them under the bed and out of the way. This also minimizes available space for growing dust bunnies under the bed!

Hack #94 – Drawer Organizers

I don't know about you, but my dresser drawers are a mess. One way to keep scarves, ties, and socks organized is to take **PVC pipe** and cut it to fit in the drawer standing on end. I stuff a pipe with a pair of socks or scarf or I coil a tie around my hand and insert it into the pipe. With the pipe ends up, I can easily see what is in there and pull it out to use it.

Hack #95 – T-Shirt Drawer

I have a lot of T-shirts and it is always a struggle to find the one I want when they are stacked on top of each other in a drawer or on a shelf. Instead of stacking them flat, I now **stack them vertically** in the drawer. I can find what I want much more easily now.

Hack #96 – Bracelet Holder

Jewelry needs a place where it can be safe but seen. I have a friend who collects massive bracelets. She stores them on a vertical **paper towel holder**, stacking them atop each other. She can see which one she wants to wear easily and just lifts it off.

Hack #97 – Pegged Rack For Jewelry Storage

A while back collapsible cup hanging racks were commonly found on kitchen walls. These expandable, adjustable racks were often made of wood and provided pegs for hanging drinking mugs by the handles. I've discovered that, in addition to making interesting wall art, these are a great way to organize necklaces and bracelets so that they're easily seen and accessed. If the rack is mounted on the wall slightly off-level, the hooks will be just enough offset from the vertical that necklaces will hang in-between the pegs below them.

Hack #98 – Egg Carton Jewelry Boxes

Another friend of mine uses paper **egg cartons** to store some of her jewelry in a drawer. You don't have to leave your egg cartons looking drab grey, either. You can paint them bright colors or glue ribbon to them to make them look more attractive.

Hack #99 – Pegboard Storage

Purchase **pegboard** from a hardware store and have it cut to fit a wall or the back of your closet door. Attach the pegboard to your wall with **strips of wood** framing behind it so the board sets out a little from the wall. Strategically place **"S" hooks and pegs** on the pegboard and use them to display purses, scarves, hats, and jewelry. Your items will be immediately accessible, even as they prettify your space.

Chapter 6: The Well-Ordered Pantry

If you are lucky enough to have a good pantry area, make the most of it. Many new houses only have cupboards and perhaps a tiny closet for a pantry. A century ago, houses were built with large pantries containing ample, shelves and bins. I lived next door to an old house and always envied my neighbor's pantry. It was the size of my adolescent bedroom. The only pantry space in my house was a tiny closet under the stairs

Even with a small kitchen, you can usually allocate a **cupboard** to storing food and call it a pantry. You can also invent space by erecting some modular or stand-alone **shelving** on one side of a room. If you want the contents to be less prominent you can always suspend a curtain, bed sheet, or tablecloth across the front.

When I lived in a postage-stamp-sized city apartment with a miniscule refrigerator, I used to stop by the market every night on the way home, so I didn't really need a pantry. However, anybody with a substantial family will need a place to store canned food, dry goods, and staples. The larger your household, the more essential is a pantry

What follows are a few ways to organize and maximize your pantry space, no matter how expansive, or dinky, it may be.

Hack #100 – Inventory Your Pantry

Inventorying your pantry is essential. Whether large or small, you want to be able to identify your pantry's contents and keep track of what needs to be used first. Everything expires. An organized pantry will help you use the oldest food first, so you don't waste anything.

One way I have found to keep track of pantry goods is to keep an inventory list. While you can maintain this on your computer, it is actually less time-intensive to keep a physical list in the pantry that you can update every time you grab a can. A paper list is okay and a chalk board or whiteboard installed on the inside door can be highly efficient. If you use a tally mark for each can, jar, or box, whenever you grab one all you need to do is mark through or erase a tally mark and you have an instantly updated inventory.

For example, I keep a supply of canned kidney beans in my pantry, along with cans of, vegetables, broth, and soups. Each of these items goes on my inventory list. When I use an item, I cross it off the list.

Let's say I have 5 cans of kidney beans, 4 cans of tomatoes, 2 cans of chicken vegetable soup. Next to each item I place hash marks representing the number of items in storage, e.g., 5 tally marks beside "kidney beans", 4 marks beside "tomatoes," etc. When I grab a can of kidney beans, I put an "X" through the hash mark on the list, or I erase a hash mark from the chalkboard or whiteboard. Either way, I know exactly how much I have.

When I get down to one or two cans, I know it's time to buy more. Before I go shopping, I refer to my inventory list to jot down what I need to buy.

Hack #101 – FIFO Pantry Organization

FIFO is geek-speak for "first in, first out." It describes an organizational system where the first item to go into storage is the first one to be removed. This is want you want for your pantry. Keep the oldest items in the front of the shelf, so you can use them first. This will keep you from wasting food by letting it expire. When you bring home more kidney beans from the store, you will put them behind the cans of beans already on the shelf. Thus, the older beans will set up front where you will naturally grab them first.

Hack #102 – Labels

I have a friend who keeps her pantry immaculate and has everything labeled. She uses a label gun to make little signs. (I'm convinced she's so organized because she just loves using that label gun!) She groups together her canned vegetables, her soups, her cereal, etc. Each row on a shelf is marked by a little label at the end telling what is in that row. My friend also keeps items in plastic bins and baskets; of course, these are labeled, too. In addition to FIFO organizing, she uses a black marker to write in bold the expiration dates on each and every can and package.

While this may sound too time-consuming for you, keep in mind that with this method of organization you pretty much only handle an item once before it is selected for use.

Hack #103 – Lazy Susan's

Lazy Susan's are wonderful for corner spaces. They allow you quick access to items that would otherwise out of reach in the deep recesses of a cabinet. A Lazy Susan allows you to turn the circular platter to get to anything you want. It reduces the number of "black holes" in your kitchen storage.

Magazine Holders

Hack #104 – A plastic or metal mesh magazine holder is a great organizer for cutting boards. Simply screw the holder to the inside of a cabinet door and your cutting boards will always be easy to reach.

Hack #105 – You can also use magazine holders to store boxes of foil, wax paper, plastic wrap, or anything in a long narrow box. Fasten a magazine rack to the back of a cupboard door with some screws or set it on a shelf with the open top of the rack facing forward for easy removal.

Hack #106 – Soda Boxes

You don't have to go out and buy expensive can holders that roll cans forward once you use the top one. Keep your 12 count soda boxes and use them to hold cans. You can paint the boxes to add durability if you like, but once they get too old and frail, just pitch them and use a fresh one.

Hack #107 – Shoe Organizers

Shoe organizers that hang from the wall or the back of a door can be used in the pantry to store just about anything. These organizers have little plastic or cloth pockets that shoes slid into. Stuff fruit snacks into one of the pockets and packages of pretzels or chips in another. Dry gravy or taco mix fits well into one of these and Kool-Aid packages are easy to find when you store them in a shoe organizer. Even small cans of tuna or tomato paste can be stored in the pockets.

Hack #108 – Juice Bottles

Save clear juice bottles or other plastic and glass jars in which to store dry goods. I keep dry beans, oatmeal, cereal, flour, and sugar in wide-mouthed glass jars. You can also store pancake mix or biscuit mix in jars; just be sure to label the containers with the directions for use. I either drop the instructions in the top of the container or tape them to the front.

Hack #109 – Container Corrals

Use plastic bins, shoeboxes, and small baskets to round up and contain small items that would otherwise spread out all over the place.

Hack #110 – Onions, Garlic And Potatoes – Hang 'em Up

Hang up non-refrigerated items in mesh bags. A cheap laundry bag works well; if it gets dirty, you just throw it in the washer. Suspend these bags from hooks. If your bag is sturdy enough hang it, not from the drawstring, but from the side so you can easily access the opening to extract what you need.

You never want your fresh items to touch the ground because that is exactly where they will rot the quickest. Hanging bags allow air to flow around all sides and will keep the items within them fresh as long as possible.

Suspend your Chips

Hack #111 – I put a plain white tension-type curtain rod at the top of my pantry inside the top shelf and hang "S" hooks on it. I clasp my bags of chips, pretzels, and noodles with a binder clip and hook it on the "S" hooks to keep the bags out of the way yet easily accessible.

Hack #112 – If you find plastic skirt hangers with the two alligator clips at either end; these also will work well for hanging chips in mid-air. Just attach a bag to the alligator clip and suspend the hanger.

Chapter 7: Laundry Tips and Tricks

I take pride in my laundry stain-fighting skills. It is an art to know what to use on which household stain. If you have kids, you know exactly what I am talking about.

Clothing isn't cheap, so the longer you can keep your clothes looking good the more wear you can get out of them. Grandma's damask tablecloth will require some special care, but the tablecloth will be passed down for generations to come no matter what gets on it, if you have a few key tricks up your sleeve. The following tips will help you know how to clean the different fabrics in your home. You will also learn tricks for getting stains out, and will know what is safe to throw in the dryer.

I've also thrown in recipes for making a few your own laundry products. These can save you money and you may well decide they work better than the commercial alternatives.

You can find more laundry hacks by watching this YouTube video called "Mom Hacks/Laundry" by WhatsUpMom.

Hack #113 – Opt For No Bleach

Bleach tends to break down the fibers of fabrics, so I do not like to use it. Instead of bleach, I use **baking**

soda for both bright colors and for whites, to keep the colors crisp. Add 1/2 cup of baking soda to your wash along with the laundry detergent.

Hack #114 – Stop Fading Colors

Turn your dark-colored clothing inside-out before throwing it into the washer. This will minimize fading.

With new clothes, treat them before you wear them. Adding 1 cup of non-iodized table **salt** to the wash will keep them from fading as quickly.

Hack #115 – Laundry Cubes

I like to make my own laundry detergent and my favorite is made in ice cube trays; they come out in little cubes. They're simple to use, non-destructive to the environment, and you know exactly what is in them. Some of my family members have detergent allergies that cause a nasty rash. However, we have had no reactions to this laundry cube recipe.

Grate a 4-ounce bar of **Castile soap** into a bowl. I use a fine cheese grater and a glass bowl, both dedicated to this purpose. Add in 1/2 cup of **washing soda**, 1/4 cup of **baking soda**, and 1/4 cup of **salt**. I use kosher salt, but you can use any salt that is non-iodized. Salt prevents colors from fading.

Slowly incorporate just enough **white vinegar** to make the mixture wet and clumpy. It will foam a bit but just keep stirring. Press the resulting mess into a plastic ice cube tray (again, dedicated for this purpose – who likes foaming ice cubes?). Really pack it in.

Set the tray in a sunny spot and let it dry for about 24 hours. The cubes will harden as they dry. When the cubes are hard, crack them out and store them in a glass jar with a tight-fitting lid. When you wash your clothes, just toss in a cube along with the clothing.

Hack #116 – Laundry Powder

Here is a recipe to use if you prefer a powder laundry detergent. A friend mixes 2 cups of grated **Castile soap**, 4 cups of **washing soda**, 4 cups of **borax,** and 2 tablespoons of **baking soda**. She adds 1/4 cup of this powder per load. This laundry powder keeps well, as long as you store it in an airtight container.

Hack #117 – Laundry Liquid

If you have a bunch of kids in the family, this laundry liquid is the way to go. It makes a batch that lasts a long time, even if you do several loads a day. You will save massive amounts of money by making this recipe. A family member with nine kids uses this all the time.

She uses Fels-Naptha soap (available in most grocery stores), but my family has allergies to this, so we use Castile soap. You will need a **five-gallon bucket** with a lid to make this laundry liquid. Grate 5.5 ounces of **Fels-Naptha or Castile soap** and put it in a pot on the stove with 4 cups of **hot water**. Cook, stirring the mixture until the soap melts. (Again, the pot and spoon should never be used for food.) Fill half of the five-gallon bucket with hot water and pour in the soap mixture. Add 1 cup of **Borax**, 1 cup of **washing soda**, and if you want, a few drops of an **essential oil,** just to make it smell good. Keep stirring as you fill the bucket almost to the top with more warm water.

My relative uses a long-handled wooden spoon to stir all the way to the bottom. Whatever you use, you don't want to immerse your hand in the liquid, unless you're wearing rubber gloves.

Put the lid on the bucket and let it set for 24 hours. When you open it, the mixture won't exactly be a liquid. It will look like a gloppy mess, but boy, does it clean! You can separate the soap into different containers, but my friend just leaves it in the bucket with the lid on and uses a measuring cup to portion out 1 cup for her top-loading washer. Front-loading washers will need only 1/2 cup of the mixture.

Hack #118 – Shrunken Clothes Fix #1

How many times have you unintentionally put something in the washer or dryer, only to discover it in the bottom, all misshapen and shrunk? To undo your mistake, soak the garment for a couple minutes in warm water, along with one small squirt of **hair conditioner**. Carefully wring out as much liquid as you can, then lay out the garment on a flat surface. Firmly stretch it back into shape and let it air dry. You may need to repeat this process several times before the garment is back to normal.

This also works with a garment that has been misshapen by stretching. Instead of pulling, you will reposition the fabric into its normal dimensions and let it dry.

Hack #119 – Shrunken Clothes Fix #2

A second method for restoring shrunken clothing involves soaking the item in lukewarm water containing a capful of **baby shampoo**. Let it soak for a while, so the shampoo has a chance to let the fibers relax. Squeeze out some of the water and lay it out flat on a beach towel. Roll the towel up with the item inside, short side to short side. This will allow the towel soak up most of the moisture. Replace the wet towel with a dry one, laying the clothing item flat as before. Gently pull the fabric back into shape. Let it air dry. This works well with jeans, as well as sweaters.

Hack #120 – Towel Freshener

Towels sometimes harbor a musty smell, even after they have been washed. To rid yourself of this odor, add 2 cups of **white vinegar** to a load of towels, along with your laundry detergent. Vinegar gets rid of nasty scents and does not leave a residual odor. I wash my towels with vinegar at least three times a year.

Hack #121 – Washer Cleaning

You wouldn't think you would have to clean your washer because you are always cleaning things in it. You will be surprised at how much better it works after you actually just clean it with no clothes in it. I do this every 3 months to keep things sparkling. **White vinegar** is what you use to clean the inside and outside of the washer. It removes stubborn soap spills and does not let mold and mildew build up in the machine.

For a **top-loading washer** run the long cycle with hot water and 4 cups of white vinegar. Let the machine agitate for 5 minutes, then stop it and let the machine sit for 1 hour. After this time, turn the washer back on and let it finish the cycle.

With a **front-loader**, again use hot water, placing 3/4 cup of white vinegar in the bleach dispenser. Run this cycle in the same way, giving it an extra rinse.

Hack #122 – Dryer Cleaning

It is probably more important that you clean your dryer than your washer. The dryer gets very hot and lint tends to accumulate in all sorts of places. If not cleaned out periodically, this lint can start a fire in the machine and in the ductwork leading outside.

You already know to clean the lint trap after every load; there might not be much there, but you still need to clean it. Anything that hinders air flow makes the machine work harder. Not only are you creating a fire hazard when you don't clean your lint trap, you also waste energy. Dryer ducts should be cleaned every six months, but this isn't hard at all to accomplish.

You should also periodically use a **lint brush** to clean out the area under the lint trap. You can find lint brushes at your local hardware store. They consist of a long spiral brush attached to a long flexible handle. Use the brush to clean out items that have collected beyond the lint trap.

I also recommend detaching your exhaust hose at least once a year and vacuuming both the inside of the hose and in the dryer's exhaust opening. For safety's sake, unplug your dryer while you clean it.

Hack #123 – Dryer Sheets

Dryer sheets are the norm in most households. They get rid of static cling and make your clothing smell nice. You aren't limited to commercial dryer sheets, however, because the alternative is easy to make and the home-made version is much cheaper.

To create your own dryer sheets, simply cut a cellulose **sponge** into half-inch strips. Close these strips in a jar, along with a little white or clear-colored **fabric softener**. Whenever you toss a load in the dryer, pull out a sponge strip, squeeze out any excess moisture, and fling it into the dryer. When your clothes are dry, fish out your little sponge strip and replace it in the jar where it will await another joyride in the dryer.

Hack #124 – Foil Static Cling ... With Foil

Because of allergies, some people are unable to use scented dryer sheets or even the sponge version. Here is an easy, nonllergenic way to rid your clothes of static cling. Roll a square of **aluminum foil** into a ball between the size of a ping pong ball and a tennis ball. Throw 2 or three of these balls in the dryer. Your clothing will come out free from static cling. It is amazing how this works to neutralize static. You can reuse them until the balls start to fall apart. Then, just make more and throw them in.

Hack #125 – Speed Up Drying Time

To speed up drying time, place a clean **dry bath towel** in with the wet clothing in your dryer. I keep older bath towels – the ones that have become a little shabby – near the dryer for this purpose. When I have a big load that might take a little longer to dry, I just throw in a dry towel. The towel absorbs some of the moisture, somehow allowing the load to dry faster and more evenly.

Hack #126 – Grease Stain Remover #1

Grease stains are insidious. Sometimes you don't know you even have them on your clothing until you wash and dry your clothes and then they jump out at you! Once an item has baked on in the dryer, the stain will always be there.

I know this is preaching to the choir, but it is important to try and treat these stains before you wash and dry the clothing. Rub a grease stain with some **blackboard chalk** and wash it normally. The grease should come right out. This sometimes works with stains that have gone through a dryer cycle, too.

Hack #127 – Grease Stain Remover #2

Another way to get grease stains out is to rub some **grease-fighting dish washing liquid** into the stain, then let it set for an hour or overnight. Wash the item as usual and the stain should come out.

Hack #128 – Ink Stains

I often use pens when I write and sometimes I find little ink marks on my clothing. When I do, I spray the marks with **hair spray** as soon as possible. I spray again ten minutes before washing. The ink usually comes out in the wash.

Hack #129 – Grass Stains

Mix 1 tablespoon of **dishwashing liquid** with 2 tablespoons of **hydrogen peroxide** in a small glass bowl. Use a white cloth to dab and rub this solution into the grass stain. Let it sit for about 15 minutes and then run cold water over it. The stain should come out and you can then launder the items normally.

Hack #130 – Red Wine Stains

I once spilled red wine on my great-grandma's white damask tablecloth and thought it was ruined for good. On a whim, I dabbed it with a white cloth soaked in **club soda** and the stain almost came out, but not completely.

After searching for remedies on the internet, I then sprinkled clean **kitty litter** on the area, rubbed the stain, and it came out completely! If you don't have kitty litter handy, I also hear the rough abrasiveness of **salt** works just as effectively.

Hack #131 – Making Whites Brighter

Throw one **aspirin** into a load of whites to keep them bright white. Don't use acetaminophen or Ibuprofen. It has to be regular, plain old aspirin.

A Word About Socks

I don't care how careful or intelligent you are, you are going to come up with odd socks periodically. It is like the washer and dryer are playing tricks on you. You can knot those socks together before throwing in the wash, but they rarely get totally clean – or dry – where the knot is. You can use a safety pin to keep sock pairs together, as long as the pin stays closed, but all that takes time I'm sure you would rather devote to something else.

Hack #132 – The best way I've found to launder socks is to use a **lingerie bag.** Just pop in all your socks, zip the bag closed, and put it through the wash. After running through the dryer, open the bag and all you need to do is match up the pairs you put in earlier.

Hack #133 – Here's one last sock tip. Always turn your socks inside-out before washing. This insures that the whole sock, even the side against your feet, is getting clean. It also helps to slow fading.

Hack #134 – Wrinkle Away

I have a habit of putting my clothes in the dryer and forgetting they are there. By the time I go to fold my clothes, some of the things are pretty wrinkled. I hate to iron; in fact, I put my iron away and forgot where I put it.

Recently, several commercial solutions to the wrinkle problem have emerged. I can't buy you a steamer, but I can offer an alternative to the commercial spray-on product that removes wrinkles. So, get your spray bottle and let's mix some up.

Mix 1/4 cup **fabric softener** with 2-1/2 cups water. You can add 1 teaspoon of **rubbing alcohol** to make it dry quicker, but I always spray my clothing the night before I need it, so I don't use the evaporative booster. Just spray this mixture on your dry clothing and smooth the clothes down with your hands. The wrinkles will fall out and go away.

Chapter 8: Ahhh! It Smells Like Home!

The basic smell of your home has much to do with how comfortable and appealing it feels. A clean, fresh scent makes a more welcome statement than the garbage convention going on in your garbage disposal or the odor of wet dog emanating from your pet.

As an alternative to commercially available room deodorizers and re-odorizers, I offer some equally effective solutions you can make fairly simply on your own; these range from potpourri to teabags! Most of these items are non-toxic and will not trigger anyone's allergies.

Hack #135 – Baking Soda And Vinegar

If you were to sniff **baking soda** (I would be careful about sniffing too hard) you would not smell much. You probably know about the tradition of putting a box of baking soda in the refrigerator to absorb odors. Baking soda soaks up bad smells and neutralizes them.

Vinegar has an acrid scent that is not all that unpleasant, but can be off-putting for some people. The thing about vinegar is that it does have that initial salad dressing smell, but as it sits, it absorbs other, more distasteful scents and leaves a "nothing" smell in its place.

Place some baking soda or vinegar in small dishes and set them in areas out of the way of children and pets. I keep a small bowl of vinegar in my bathroom and it keeps away the litter box smell, among other odors. This won't add scent to your home, but it will neutralize less attractive smells.

Hack #136 – Garbage Disposal

The garbage disposal is easily a major source of offensive household odors. Nothing is worse than anticipating an at-home feeling after a long day away, only to being walloped by a garbagy malodor as you enter your kitchen. It's even worse when you realize the stench is coming from your sink.

Eat an orange or cook with a lemon and toss the **peels** in your garbage disposal to freshen it. I keep some peels in zip-lock bags in the refrigerator or freezer and use them throughout the week. I never keep them longer than four days in the refrigerator but find that they seem to keep their freshness as long as they stay cold. If you freeze fruit rinds, they last longer and it doesn't hurt to put them down the garbage disposal while frozen. Just run that disposal and get rid of the nasty smell.

Hack #137 – The Vinegar Fix

Vinegar also will deodorize your garbage disposal. Throw a few **ice cubes** in along with a squirt or two of white or apple cider vinegar and churn away. The ice cubes will dislodge anything stuck to the blades and the vinegar will kill the germs and help break down greasy buildup.

Hack #138 – Lemon And Orange Aromatherapy

Citrus fruits give off a lovely clean scent that is pleasing to the senses. Cut a lemon or orange in half. Juice it and use the juice in cooking. Sprinkle about one tablespoon of **sea salt** on the inside of the **peel** along with a few **whole cloves**. Place them in a bowl and leave them around the house where pets and children cannot reach them. The salt enhances the scent and also keeps the skins from rotting quickly. Once they stop giving off their pleasant aroma, it is time to throw the peels away and start with a new batch.

Hack #139 – Vent Air Freshening

You know those cute little deodorizers you clip onto the vents in your car? You can use them in your house, too. Just clip them to the air vents. The air coming through the vents will push the scent out into the house and get rid of any staleness.

Hack #140 – Make Your Own Bamboo Diffuser

You have seen those pretty bamboo diffusers with a pretty jar or bottle and bamboo sticks sticking out. The scented liquid in the bottle soaks in and travels up the bamboo to infuse your home with a lovely scent. They can be quite expensive, but you don't have to spend a lot of money on them. Instead, you can make your own for a fraction of the price. You start with a **bottle** that has a fairly small opening. It can be large or small, plain or highly decorated. Just select something you will enjoy having around.

For the **fragrance**, you can use citrus-scented cleaning solution, you can buy commercial fragrance blends, or you can make your own from the instructions for a general cleaner found at the beginning of this book. In fact, you can add any scent you want to this mixture. Lavender or lilac is always nice, but if you want something a little stronger, you can use rose.

For infusers, use **bamboo shish-kabob skewers** and trim off the points with scissors. The skewers should be two times the height of the fragrance container, so if your jar is 8 inches tall, the skewers need to be 16 inches tall.

I have used a 6-inch tall glass apothecary bottle with 12 inch skewers. Making your own is much less expensive than buying a ready-made diffuser. You can easily tailor the scent to your needs and preferences.

Hack #141 – Eucalyptus Treatment

Eucalyptus has a strong scent that some might say is antiseptic. The scent tends to clear the sinuses. I happen to love the smell however, even when I don't have a stuffy head cold. That said, hanging a sprig of eucalyptus in or near the shower where it won't get all wet, will scent the bathroom when you take a shower. The steam releases the oils into the room. It can definitely clear your head in the morning, as well as making the room smell very pleasant.

Hack #142 – Scent Your Home With Dryer Sheets

Dryer sheets come in a bunch of different scents and you can use them to scent the entire house. Pop off the cover of your heating vents, lay a dryer sheet over the back side of the vent, and pop it back on. The dryer sheet will be behind the vent. Since dryer sheets are manufactured to take the heat, they should not cause a problem. The heated air in the winter will flow through the drier sheet and invisibly scent the room. While the manufacturer makes no claims to this effect, dryer sheets may also trap and prevent floating debris from entering both the room and your lungs as you inhale.

Hack #143 – Scent Your Lingerie Drawer

Dryer sheets and **sachets** (We'll cover them in a little bit) can also add fragrance to dresser drawers and their contents. They will scent your clothing, so that you'll enjoy putting them on.

Hack #144 – Essential Oils And Light Bulbs

I must have 20 little bottles of essential oils in a variety of different scents. These come in very handy to scent my house. You can take a cotton swab and wet it with an essential oil. While your lamp is off, smear some of the essential oil on your light bulb. When you turn the lamp on, the essential oil will grow warm and dissipate the scent into the environment.

Hack #145 – Essential Oils And Cotton Balls

Another way to use **essential oils** to scent the house is to lightly soak a **cotton ball** in the oil and place it in a small dish. Set this dish out of the way and it will continue to scent your home for up to a week. I use a shallow bowl and set it on top of the books in my living room bookshelf. It keeps the room smelling lovely.

Hack #146 – Essential Oils And The Furnace

You are supposed to change your **furnace filter** periodically, so when you do, scatter 10 drops of your favorite **essential oil** on the fresh filter before you pop it into the furnace. The oils will scent the home for quite a long time and will circulate through the entire house.

Hack #147 – Essential Oils And Pine Cones

I love the rustic look of pine cones, especially in the winter and during the holidays. There's no reason you can't have a few pine cones strategically placed in baskets around the house any time of the year. The petals of the pine cone are dry and they hold on to essential oils very nicely without having to add a fixative.

Just sprinkle some drops on some big pine cones and set them in a basket. I love to sprinkle mine with cinnamon oil during the holidays, but you can use any scent you like. The only problem is that you have to stay with the same scent. Like I said, pine cones hold on to those scents for a very long time.

Hack #148 – Coffee

Coffee is one of those scents that almost everyone likes. Grind some **coffee beans** to release the aroma and put the fresh grounds in a small bowl in an out-of-the-way place. The only problem with this is you'll want to drink coffee all the time!

Hack #149 – Tea

Tea has the ability to neutralize nasty odors in the same way as baking soda. Pour some **loose tea leaves** in a bowl and leave them around the house in smelly areas to absorb and neutralize odors. You can also add 1/4 cup of loose black tea to the bottom of your cat's litter box and pour litter over it. Periodically give the litter box a shake to prolong the fresh smell.

Hack #150 – Cinnamon Sticks

Cinnamon sticks carry a pleasant odor that is strong enough to mask nasty smells. Break some **cinnamon sticks** in half or crush them with a hammer and put the pieces in a bowl in an out-of-the-way place. You can also add a little **cinnamon**, **ginger**, or **nutmeg essential oil** to the sticks. They do not need a fixative and will function much like the pine cones.

Hack #151 – Stovetop Potpourri

Boiling something on the stove is an age-old way of making your house smell good. A stovetop potpourri can be made out of common ingredients added to water. You just set a small pot of **water** on the stove to boil and it releases a pleasant scent that permeates the house. The only problem is that once you stop boiling, the smell dissipates rather quickly. If you start the pot to simmering 15 minutes before guests arrive, your house will smell wonderful when they open the door.

Cinnamon sticks and whole **cloves** make for a spicy potpourri. You can also boil **citrus peel** to give off lemony or orange freshness. A couple sprigs of **lavender, eucalyptus, or mint** can make your house smell fresh. If you want to build anticipation for a mouthwatering dinner, raid your spice cabinet again. **Marjoram, sage, garlic**, and even **bullion** can stimulate a ravenous appetite.

Hack #152 – Homemade Household Scents

Make your own delightful household spray by filling a spray bottle with 4 ounces of **distilled water** and 10 to 20 drops of your favorite **essential oil**. Mix by shaking well each time before you spray it.

Hack #153 – Dry Potpourri

Potpourri is an age-old method for freshening the air around us. The smells in the Middle Ages were pretty raw and people were always interested masking them with something more pleasant. Back then, people would strew herbs across their floors. Whenever a person walked across the floor, they would crush the herbs underfoot, releasing a fresh scent to cover up other nasty odors in the room.

Victorian ladies often held small nosegays of dried flowers or carried scented handkerchiefs as they walked about. These they would sniff whenever the scents of the day grew a little too strong. Dry potpourri is an offshoot of these older methods of refreshing the air we breathe.

Everything used in a dry potpourri must be completely dry, except for the essential oils. Any moisture will cause the potpourri to mold and generate less-than-pleasant odors.

You can use **dried flowers**, **herb leaves,** and **dried spices** to make your own potpourri. The most popular ingredients are dried rose petals or rosebuds, lavender buds, cinnamon sticks, cloves, thyme leaves, and eucalyptus leaves.

Some dried material does not have a scent, but is included because it is visually pleasing. The aim is to make something that looks as good as it smells. All kinds of flower petals are easily dried to use in potpourri. Try some unscented straw flowers, German statice flower, or amaranth to add color to your mixture. These flowers grow almost dry to begin with; they just need a little time to completely dry after cutting.

Any kind of herb leaf works well in potpourri and so do the dried leaves of **scented geraniums**. Scented geraniums come in a wide variety of fragrances that stay with the leaves after they dry.

Potpourri requires a **fixative**, something that will hold on to the scent and slow its evaporation. As a fixative, I use about one tablespoon of **orris root** per potpourri batch. Orris root is a powdery substance that absorbs any essential oil you put into your potpourri and sustains its essence for a long time. You can also use **cinnamon** (ground or stick) as a fixative. **Nutmeg, coriander**, and **cumin** are other fixatives you may already have in your kitchen. Just put everything together in a sealed bag for a couple weeks to let the fragrance permeate your mixture, before placing it out to decorate both the appearance and the breathing quality of your rooms.

If you have cats or dogs, you will need to prevent your potpourri from being eaten. I place mine in small mason jars and cut a square of nylon net fabric placing it over the opening of the jar as I screw on the ring. My animals cannot get to the potpourri, but the scent can waft freely through my rooms.

Hack #154 – Gel Air Fresheners

Make your own gel air fresheners and put them in small mason jars to set about the house. They are super easy to make and if you are afraid of pets trying to eat them, just place a piece of nylon net over the opening with a metal ring screwed on the jar to hold it in place.

Protect your skin before you begin the gel-making process, as the chemicals can burn your skin. Begin by pouring 1 cup of **water** into a saucepan and heating it until it boils. Turn off the heat and sprinkle 1 ounce of **gelatin** over the top. With a whisk, stir the liquid until the gelatin is completely dissolved.

Add 1 tablespoon of **salt** and 2 cups of cold tap water. Whisk the contents again and set the mixture aside. Put 20 drops of an **essential oil** into the jar. Pour the gel mixture into the jar while it is still hot, filling it up to less than an inch from the rim. Add some **food coloring** if desired and stir this in as well.

Place the jar on a heatproof surface and let it set until completely cool. Then you can secure a piece of nylon net over the opening and place it out to freshen the air. This gel freshener will last for 3 to 4 weeks, depending on environmental factors. Beyond a month it tends to get moldy, so I recommend discarding the contents earlier, washing out the jars, and when you have enough empty jars accumulated, make another batch.

Hack #155 – Sachets

Sachets are little fabric pillows filled with potpourri. They are an ideal use for your dry potpourri. The good thing about a sachet is that the potpourri is contained inside a little pouch. You can cut two squares of fabric and sew the items inside of them or just place potpourri in the center of a large square and bring up all the sides to tie it closed with knot, a ribbon, or some string.

Place sachets in your drawers or hang them from a clothes hanger in a closet to keep your clothing smelling nice. You can put a sachet in the pantry, in your shoes, in the bathroom, or anywhere else you would like to freshen the air.

You can use almost any fabric, but it must be loosely woven in order to let out the scent. I like to use muslin because of its loose weave and the availability of multiple colors. You can also use loosely woven cotton. If you sew well, make a drawstring casing on one edge and lace it with ribbon to close the little pillow. You can refresh the potpourri inside at any time, by just opening it up, pouring out the old stuff, and replacing it with fresh potpourri.

Hack #156 – Fabric Freshener Spray

Don't spend lots of money on fabric fresheners when you can make one that works effectively on upholstery, clothing, carpet, and rugs. In a spray bottle, combine 1/8 cup clear or white liquid **fabric softener** with 2 teaspoons of **baking soda**. Fill the bottle to near the top with warm tap water and shake it so that the baking soda dissolves. This fabric freshener will keep for several weeks and you only need to spray it lightly on fabric items to give them a fresh smell.

Chapter 9: Money and Lifestyle Hacks

You can save a great deal of money by using the tips that follow.

It almost goes without saying that by making the various cleaning and refreshing solutions mentioned in this book, you'll save a considerable amount of money. A bottle of Swiffer wet-jet cleaning fluid usually costs you about $3.50, but if you make it yourself and repeatedly reuse the container, you are probably spending about $.50 per bottle. A good spray carpet spot cleaner can cost you five to nine dollars, but if you make it yourself, you will only spend a few cents. Laundry detergent can set you back $18 for a big bottle, but making your own laundry cubes will cost only a few bucks.

The following are a few other ways to save money by around the home. We'll start with how you handle money and then move on to other lifestyle hacks that can save you a ton.

Hack #157 – Use Bill-Pay

You can actually save quite a bit of money when you opt to pay bills monthly with an automated system through their program. Some companies assess a charge if you pay through your bank or by check but are happy to extract what you owe them if you give them access to your bank account. The only catch:

money has to be in the bank when the bill comes due. If your bill is due on the fifteenth of the month and you are paid monthly, instead of two times a month, you will need to carefully monitor your bank balance and leave enough in your account for these regular payments. Otherwise, bank fees can easily far outstrip any savings this will give you.

Most banks now offer online bill-paying systems. This is ideal if your income varies. You can easily set up a reminder through your bank to tell you it's time to pay a specific bill. Then you can schedule your online payment for when there's adequate money in the bank.

Hack #158 – Check Bill Statements And Bank Statements

You would be surprised how many erroneous charges you can find in bills and bank statements. I once discovered several calls on my phone bill that could not have been made by me. They amounted to a sizeable sum of money. Fortunately, because I noticed them early, I was able to call the phone company and have the charges removed.

The same thing can happen with your credit card. If you check each credit card statement when it arrives, you will be able to recognize errant charges while your memory is fresh enough to dispute them. I've caught errors and saved myself a lot of money this way.

Hack #159 – Pay Ahead

Many insurance companies will allow you to pay for six months to a year in advance, saving significant overhead charges this way. If you can afford to pay ahead, do it.

Hack #160 – Minimize Interest Rates

Always submit your credit card payments on time. If you don't, that low APR you signed up for may disappear.

Watch the rates associated with your accounts and don't feel bad about switching cards if you find a company that will approve you for a lower interest rate. Companies don't think twice about raising your rates, so you should not be concerned about leaving them if you find something better. This also applies to insurance and cell phone service.

Once a year, I review all my banking and service rates. I prowl online, seeking the best rates on each service. If I like a current service provider, I will give them the opportunity to match any competitor's rate before I commit to switching. Given the chance, many companies will adjust their rate, just to keep a paying customer from leaving.

Hack #161 – Use Cold Water

Use cold water to wash your laundry. This will save you a boatload of money because you no longer have to pay the gas company to heat your water. Colored clothing does much better in cold water anyway, minimizing fading and color bleeds. When you use cold water, you usually don't need to worry about mixing colors with whites and your detergent should work just as effectively. The only time you should use warm or hot water is to deal with certain stains, as we've already mentioned.

Hack #162 – Wash Full Loads

Only run the dishwasher and washing machine when you have full loads. You are wasting the money when you pay both to operate the machine and for the water used. Your machine can't tell the difference between washing 2 pieces or 20 and it is going to take the same amount of energy for both amounts.

Hack #163 – Air Dry

Use the air-dry cycle on your dishwasher instead of drying with heat. That heat-dry setting can drive up your electric bill like crazy. You should also air dry clothing on a clothesline outside if you can. While it takes a little longer to hang the clothes, it will save you money on running the dryer and you will get the added bonus of fresh-smelling clothes.

Hack #164 – Unplug To Save

Always unplug unused appliances when you are not using them. How many digital clocks do you need to sustain, anyhow? And those little red LEDs used to show that your appliances are on stand-by? Guess what. They use electrical energy to tell you they're in energy-saving mode!

Unplug your toaster, coffee-maker, and phone charger when they are not in use. Some people say that unplugging things doesn't matter, but I saw a definite difference in my electric bill when I unplugged items until I needed to use them.

Hack #165 – Fill Your Freezer

Freezers work more efficiently when they are full. They require less energy to sustain a freezing temperature. If your freezer is only partially full, I suggest you fill it with something. I take gallon jugs, fill them with cold water, and place them in the freezer to fill up the empty space and conserve energy.

Hack #166 – Heat Water Optimally

Keep the temperature on your water heater no higher than 120 degrees F. Any higher and the water heater will use more energy than you want to pay for. Any lower and you just may have a cold shower in the morning.

Hack #167 – Close Closet Doors

This might sound silly, but, keep the doors to your closets closed. If they are open, your furnace and air conditioner will spend extra energy (and your money) trying to regulate a room you rarely enter. Experts estimate that you can save $50 or more just by keeping those closet doors shut.

Hack #168 – Pick Your Batteries

Use rechargeable batteries in toys, remote controls, and other battery-powered items. The only thing to use a single-use battery in is your smoke detector. Even that can be hard-wired into your house so you don't need to spend money on new batteries.

Hack #169 – Change Air Filters

The air filters in your furnace and your air conditioning unit need to be changed at least once per quarter. If you don't change out your filters, air will be constricted throughout these systems, making them more costly to run. In addition, frequently clean the filters in your washer, dryer and dishwasher. Not only will this save money, it will also help minimize wear and tear on their motors and – in the case of your dryer – the danger of fire.

Hack #170 – Avoid Processed Foods

Processed and pre-packaged foods tend to cost more than buying the ingredients and making them yourself. Eating fresh foods makes more sense to your health and your pocketbook. You can buy a large can of applesauce for about $3; it will give you about six servings. If you buy the same amount of applesauce in individual snack-sized portions, you will pay double in most cases. Instead, pour that big jar of applesauce into individual portion-sized airtight plastic containers and take a serving at a time to lunch. Sure, you'll have to lug the container around, bring it home, and wash it before using it again, but just think of all the money you're saving and all the plastic that is *not* going into landfills!

Hack #171 – Grow Your Own Food

You can save money year-round by growing your own food. For what you can't grow, buy items when they are in season. Strawberries are cheap during the spring because, in most cases, they can be grown locally. Once December comes around, they are much more expensive because they are out of season and have to be trucked in. When you grow your own food, you can make the harvest last by freezing or canning it for use in the off-months.

Hack #172 – Pack Your Lunch

A good way to save money is to pack your lunch when you go to work or school. You can get insulated bags that keep food cold or hot. Buying lunch at a fast food joint would cost you upwards of six dollars, where a packed lunch will cost less than half that amount.

Hack #173 – Make Restaurant Meals Special

It is always nice to go out to eat, but watch how many times you eat out in a month. It is much cheaper to prepare your own food. Besides, if you seldom eat out, when you *do* go out to eat, the occasion will be all the more special. I would prefer to save up and go once a month to a really nice restaurant, than to eat out every day at a cheap fast-food joint.

You can always prepare meals ahead, for those times you just don't feel like cooking. Take a weekend and prepare several meals. Freeze them in meal-sized portions and later you can take them out to thaw well before you want to eat them.

If you do decide to have friends over and would normally meet at a restaurant, invite them to your place to make dinner together, instead. Ask your friends to bring their own ingredients to add to the feast. It's much more fun – and it's easier on the budget – to cook together and eat what you made.

Hack #174 – Save With Store Brands And Generic Foods

Store brands and generic foods are often just as tasty as brand names. Of course, we all have our individual tastes. I like a certain kind of ketchup and no other brand will do, but when it comes to macaroni and cheese, one box is just as good as another, in my opinion. Just compare the two brands to ensure you get the same amount of food for your money.

Hack #175 – Shun Vending Machines

Stay away from the vending machines at work or school. A can of pop is about $1.25 from a vending machine where a case of 12 might cost you five or six dollars at the grocery store. That's a huge difference. A four-dollar bag of chips can be divided into six or more individual portions, while a little bag from the machine will cost nearly a dollar.

Hack #176 – Better Than Bottled Water

You can buy bottled water on sale and save money that way, but it is even better to attach a water filter to your faucet and fill a high-quality reusable water bottle. You save money and, like I said before, less plastic ends up in our landfills.

Hack #177 – Use Coupons

Use coupons whenever you can. Some stores offer to double your coupons. Others will match the deals of their competitors. Check your local newspaper, store circulars, and the internet for coupons.

Coupons are also good for a lot more than just groceries. You can realize savings on office supplies, computer equipment, clothing, diapers, cleaning supplies and just about anything else with coupons. Don't forget about restaurant coupons, either. Some communities have a website you can visit to buy a half-off coupon for specific items. My community offers a free dinner at a local restaurant if you buy one for $12. You have to purchase your dinner from the website, but you get a voucher for the free meal.

Hack #178 – Use Store Circulars

Always check store circulars that appear weekly in your newspaper or in the mail. At my house, we build our weekly menu around the deals in the circulars; we limit our purchases to sale items for most of our dinners.

Hack #179 – Optimize Shopping Trips

When you are ready to go to the grocery store, go equipped with a shopping list; if you take a list with you, you'll be a lot less likely to impulse buy, spending money unnecessarily

In my household, I figure out the menu for at least one week. I write down everything I need to buy for each meal as well as for sack lunches, breakfasts and snacks. As I write down each item, I group it with other items I'll find in the same section of the store.

I then take this shopping list to the store and rarely deviate from it. Buying things you don't need just because they caught your eye is when you can get into trouble. Avoid buying foods your body doesn't need, like cookies and candies. They will drive up your food bill and expand your waistline.

When you get everything you need in a single trip you save money, because you won't be using gas – and time – running to the store again. Neither will you be tempted again by enticing store displays into buying extras you don't need.

I first go to a store where the items are the least expensive. I then go to the next-best store to find everything else. I make it a habit to visit no more than three stores in a single shopping trip; more than that and I'm just wasting any money I would otherwise have saved on gas.

Hack #180 – Go To Resale Stores

You can often find quite serviceable furniture and decor at a resale store. I even buy clothing and some gifts at resale stores, especially when they still have the store price tags on them. Goodwill, Salvation Army, and Habitat for Humanity's Restore are just a few places you can find high quality items for a really good price. Consignment stores sell primarily high quality clothing, along with a few other items. They can also be a good source for quality pre-owned items.

I have one friend who buys every stitch of her children's clothing from a Restore, because the kids grow out of things so quickly. She returns clothing that hasn't been ripped or stained and gets store credit with which she buys additional clothing.. My friend has also been able to find nearly-new children's shoes, playpens, beds, toys, high chairs, swings, and such, all for less than half price.

Most of these stores ensure that items are completely clean before displaying them. I feel perfectly safe with the things I have bought. The only things I won't buy secondhand are bedding and underwear.

Hack #181 – Toy And Clothing Swaps

If you can't find one where you live, I recommend organizing a toy and clothing swap in your community. Arrange to hold this activity in a community center or at your church. A swap allows people to bring in gently used toys and clothing to swap out for other toys and clothing. This is a good way to recycle items that have more life in them while saving money.

Hack #182 – Rethink Cable TV

Cable TV is expensive. Instead of paying that money to your local cable company, ensure that you have internet access and Wi-Fi, then hook your television up to Netflix, Hulu, Google Plus or another pay-as-you-go service. Paying for Netflix and Hulu is much cheaper than paying for cable and you can still watch any of your favorite TV shows.. If you are an Amazon Prime subscriber, you can watch movies and TV shows either free or at a reduced price. You may have to wait until after the cable airing to watch current episodes, but the savings is well worth the wait in my book.

You can still watch your local channels by installing an antenna. I have an HDTV antenna that sticks to the window. It picks up all our local stations, along with PBS and a few other stations I didn't know existed.

You can save $100 to $200 a month by getting rid of cable TV and paying as you go. You will still be able to enjoy the shows you like, but you can watch them on *your* schedule, not just when they are broadcast.

Hack #183 – Stash Your Change

The last tip I have for you is to collect all the change you gather in your coat pockets, your pants pockets, your purse, and your car. Put it all in a big jar. When the jar gets full, count your coins or take them to the bank and have a cashier count them for you. You will be surprised at how much change you have collected! Then give yourself a special treat with the money you've saved. Or give it to someone in need.

I have a relative who stashes the coins she finds from cleaning the apartments she manages. Once a year she uses the coins to fund a weekend in Vegas. That's her idea of fun. What's yours?

Conclusion

I hope this book was able to help you discover new ways to keep your home clean and neat, save money on cleaning materials, and make your home environmentally safe. The next step is to make your own cleaning solutions and start using the easy life hacks in this book.

Make the rooms in your house a safe haven for friends and family by using these nontoxic and common-sense hacks for the household. They save you money, are safe for pretty much everyone, and are super easy to make and use. You should have no problem whipping up a batch of laundry tablets or making your own scrubbing bubbles using inexpensive items you may already have in your kitchen. There is no need to introduce unwanted chemicals into your home, because you now know the natural way to clean. You have also discovered ways to save money in your home, from closing closet doors to simplifying your bill-paying.

I hope you've been able to affirm some things you're already doing well; for these parts of your life, go ahead and implement any minor tweaks you've seen that can optimize both your health and your pocketbook. Of course, it can be overwhelming to change everything at once. Just like any habit, it's best to change only a couple things at first. Get yourself used to making your own dish detergent, for example, then gradually start swapping out your cleaning solutions for home-made alternatives, one by one. Give yourself – and your family – time to adjust to one change before adding another. Pick and choose the hacks you implement based on your needs. Before long, you will have optimized your entire lifestyle.

Finally, if you discovered at least one thing that has helped you or that you think would be beneficial to someone else, be sure to take a few seconds to easily post a quick positive review. As an author, your positive feedback is desperately needed. Your highly valuable five star reviews are like a river of golden joy flowing through a sunny forest of mighty trees and beautiful flowers! *To do your good deed in making the world a better place by helping others with your valuable insight, just leave a nice review.*

My Other Books and Audio Books
www.AcesEbooks.com

Popular Books

RECIPE BOOK

The Best Food Recipes
That Are Delicious, Healthy,
Great For Energy And Easy To Make

Ace McCloud

CROCKPOT RECIPES
THE TOP 100 BEST SLOW COOKER RECIPES OF ALL TIME
ACE MCCLOUD

GLUTEN FREE

YOUR COMPLETE GUIDE TO THE HEALTHIEST GLUTEN
FREE FOODS ALONG WITH DELICIOUS & ENERGIZING
GLUTEN FREE COOKING RECIPES

Ace McCloud

ULTIMATE HEALTH SECRETS

HEALTH

Strategies For Dieting, Eating Healthy, Exercising,
Losing Weight, The Mediterranean Diet,
Strength Training, And All About Vitamins,
Minerals, And Supplements

Ace McCloud

LOSE WEIGHT

**THE TOP 100 BEST WAYS
TO LOSE WEIGHT QUICKLY AND HEALTHILY**

Ace McCloud

Ace McCloud

HABIT

The Top 100 Best Habits
How To Make A Positive Habit Permanent
And How To Break Bad Habits

Be sure to check out my audio books as well!

 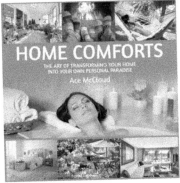 

Check out my website at: www.AcesEbooks.com for a complete list of all of my books and high quality audio books. I enjoy bringing you the best knowledge in the world and wish you the best in using this information to make your journey through life better and more enjoyable! **Best of luck to you!**

9 781640 481688